ON MOUNTAINS' BREATH

Harold Littlebird

Tooth of Time
Books
1982

Acknowledgements

Some of these poems have previously appeared in the following magazines and anthologies:

New Mexico Review, New Mexico Magazine, Alcheringa, Pembroke Magazine, Coyote's Journal, Voices of the Rainbow, Voices of the Rio Grande, Southwest, Indian Rio Grande, The Remembered Earth and *The Greenfield Review*.

With special thanks to Barbara, who edited these writings.

ISBN: 0-940510-03-0

For my daughters Elima, Chamisa and Maya: and most of all, for Barbara, who makes it all complete.

CONTENTS

Our Father the Sun, has given to all people his radiant light
to remind mankind of their humility
His is the path we follow throughout our lifetimes
to know when it is proper for all our earthly doing
planting, hunting, bearing children
to know where there is the sustenance of water, roots and animals
look carefully at how we love this life
and how our Mother Earth remembers her children

LORENZO'S SONG

there is singing
song in motion
in simple melody
high through the heavens and in the space between
sky and earth are you
growing and vibrant and unique
and in your growing there is your brother, Elk Rider
your sisters, *Hay-a-shee, Dya-tza-ah*
all from the mountains and sky
and from this you stem
you whose Indian name I can't remember but know your singing
there in the grey house surrounding you that knew your beginning
in your cradle of oak swaying
and outward to the brown-grey land and alfalfa fields
to the river swollen in Spring, flowing and rolling swiftly
and beyond
in that current of life all around
from the smallest flower your existence began
a seedling alive and growing
in its rightful place
blessed by spirits of wind and water
taking hold to its mother
sucking from the womb of the earth
whispering unseen
giving thanks for its being
from this you came happily
one crisp morning in the dark of the new moon

bonding and adding strength to your mother and father
both of whom I know and love as you
it is from this and more that you are now a year and growing
it is from legends and stories and songs listened to and lived by
that messengers in the night will tell you in your dreaming
you will carry, learn and share
and it is from this and more that you are growing
more than I can say with words
it is in the likeness of breaths on corn pollen
and silent prayer to holy things on the fourth morning
and all of this I know you singing, eyes shining
and simply caring in your mountain home!

FOR THE GIRLS CAUSE THEY KNOW

goodnight, my two little cloud ladies
Elima, *Tzina-dhy-duoay,* fat dark rain bearer
you are the echoes of summer
flooding of rivers
shaping of arroyos
the tears in my eyes
Chamisa, *Hena-dhay,* gentle misty lady rain
you bring a joy to the fields
the answer of prayers for the corn,
the melons, the chili and me
my two dark children
carrying a sorrow and strength
bring to us the lasting peace
we all once knew

A BIRTHDAY WISH FOR MY COLORADO LADY

Colorado Lady in my sunshine dreaming
Lady blossom in my life re-newing
Lady of mountain and windy sky
you share the color of the billowy clouds
woven in your flowing brown hair
tossed gently in April's breathing
Spring is upon you, all fresh, all new
and you are Spring bringing flower and fruit
carrying with you the seed of this new year
Lady of life, Lady of Happiness, Lady of mine

Waiting out the winter in our home
warm from cedar and oak fire
watching you day by day grow with child
reminiscing, last winter at Camel Rock in the night
with my daughters and stars and high thin clouds,
on the Pecos River eating hot dogs with Bruce and Adrianna
in early Spring
'til now, becoming parents, longing for this baby
you asked me once what sort of child I wanted
I didn't answer but thought
I want a baby full of you and me
born out of the love we give
blessed by mountains and sun
cradled first in your womb
and then in our arms and hearts
I want a strong baby full of summer clouds
embraced by bright flowers blooming

if it be a she-child
then let her know things in simple beauty and caring
let us teach her quietly in soft praying
let us teach her kindness for all things
tenderness is her birthright
and prepare her as parental guardians
and give her a mellow name to be guided by
and the earth and sky will know her

if it be a he-child
let him know the Earth as Mother and Sun as Father
let us teach him kindness and caring and patience
his will be full male cloud and thunder
I will show him hunting and those stories
and sing him the songs and dances
he will grow beside us lending his joy

this is the child I want, a daughter or son
surrounded by ancestry
respectful and full of rememberance
a strong healthy child ripe of Winter's song
born into summer warmth
a gift of seed from me nurtured by you

this then is the child I pray
laughing for the sun and rain
running like the mountain streams
carrying on that which we cherish
loved by old mountain clouds
blessed by dry arroyo air and soft summer breathing
growing content and enduring

NEW MOON DAUGHTER

June 23, 1977

in the late night of a new moon you come forth
squirming and reaching, the color that is before dawn
entering from another world
quickly changing from blue to yellow to bright peach orange
and begin to breathe your new realm
a whimper from your tiny mouth then calmness
laying on your mother's belly, sucking on her breast
small body pulsing long and slow
child, you grasp with fragile hands and arms,
blessing us over and over
soon you will be presented to the sky and earth
your name will remind all of us who you are
sleep now, little one, sleep and dream for the people

fourth day

it is your grandmother from Paguate that gives you *Gowe-na-tza*
daughter, this is how we'll know you
your mother and I chose for you Bluebird, but your grandma and
grandpa couldn't remember how it was spoken
and on your fourth afternoon, because we could not decide sooner,
you have our given name, Maya Juanita Littlebird
Maya, like the ancient and wise empire of Central America
Maya, like a song, soft and subtle
Juanita, because you almost came on San Juan Feast
Maya Juanita, daughter bringing joy, one week old

hummingbird
magenta-green and white
carrier of light and wind
from the south you came singing
a high shrill whistle weighted with rain
everywhere you flew the grasses bowed in prayer
and a greeness came to the land as your song was heard
your wings rushed the clouds
bringing sweet wet seed from the skies
and everywhere you looked was singing

A CIRCLE BEGINS

in the surround of snow-touched mountains
a circle begins
in a meadow by a snow melt creek
where hands weave a house of thin green saplings
   it is a way of song
    a way of breathing
a pure womb to center oneself through sweat
a way of blessing and being blessed
a circle of humility, prayer and asking
and there are no clocks to measure time
but the beating of our singing hearts

INDEPENDENCE PASS

mountains snow covered and glowing
in the afternoon's brilliance
air thick of pine and pitch
springs erupting from cracks
in the sides of rough granite land flows
gushing and pumping the life-blood of the earth mother
far to the valleys below
and the peaks towering like sentries
high into the clouds and further
and the fullness and wonder and serene beauty
this pass called Independence
surrounded in awe, wide-eyed and reverent
like the time in Utah, at sweat, with Bruce and Adrianna
the all-mother came and washed me
blessing with air and cold and I sang in solemn laughter
and my thoughts were of home
and my dad's father and his father before him
the language to describe this wholeness and being a part of it
one part in many
my heart was pounding mountain summer
asking to breathe, taste and share
like dancing and the cottonwood drum
every muscle and vein was taut and swollen
intent on moving without strain, bursting forth
for the people in harmony and song
the wind gusting, trees swaying
springs running, grasses growing
snow covering, the earth living . . .
these and more I know my father and his father
and his father's father danced
and my father has let it be known to me
up there is prayer without words
surrounded by spirits of caring
and the tears in my eyes were for knowing
that's from where I come
and that's where song and motion and language is born and re-born
and the sound from any one person is power re-called
and should be held in deepest respect and mystery
for it is sacred like breath itself

FOR DRUM HADLEY

oh, thank you, cowboy with four-wheel drive
for bringing us here
where the hills are worked by erosion
and the sands sing songs to the silvery clouds
where ducks form V's as they fly overhead
and short clear cut whistles are heard as they wing on by
oh thank you cowboy, standing there
where yucca and cedar are everywhere you look
and the air smells thick of sage
oh thank you cowboy, with four-wheel drive
for sharing with me the breezes of the crisp winter sky
and walking the arroyos where every curve is rounded
by melting snow
and a lone cock pheasant croos in the distance
oh thank you cowboy, with big white stetson and red handkerchief
for being in this parched Chimayo land
where my rifles' voice makes songs against the ever-changing
red rock mesas
oh thank you, bearded cowboy
for tasting this day together
with its rocks and arroyos and stubby pinon trees
this is where we are cowboy, and where we'll always be . . .
with the land
oh, thank you, Drum
for bringing us home

AFTER THE POW-WOW

(an excerpt)

I tell him how it used to be in Paguate
before the Jackpile Uranium mine opened,
the way my mother remembers it
She would say: *"That's when there was still farming*
through the valley and on up the canyon;
the peach trees and rows of corn, melon patches and
fields of grain and wheat where the mine is now.
That was when it was still a long ways from the village."
And how she said not too many Paguate men worked there yet,
now it is an ugly scar just east of the village
across the two-laned highway
And the mill tailings are left uncovered,
blown about by the winds,
with no provisions for removal and no one in authority
seems to care.
How the people were told to build the foundations of their
new houses with the tailings and how they used this excess
to line the roads to hold the dust down
In the community buildings where some ceremonies are held,
the dirt floor is mixed with these tailings.
Now there are more cases of cancer, birth defects and
internal disorders in the elderly;
and more up-dated statistics on how to get more uranium
with modern equipment brought in by large oil companies
like Exxon, Shell, Amoco.

The People are caught in a catch-22
They have to work in order to live, and the mine is there,
the money keeps coming, and the people keep working
under unhealthy and dangerous conditions;
and so the songs will continue.
It's not his fault I know, so I sip my coke and
change the subject
and we continue to talk about traveling
but I will remember to sing for him also.

The preceeding excerpt is taken from a narrative describing a chance conversation which
took place in the Los Angeles International Airport, between myself and a representative
of a large oil company with mineral holdings in New Mexico. I was returning from a
Pow-wow in Davis, California.

moonlight, moon bright
guide us safely through the night
you are what we all come from
keep us from all worldly harm
moon bright, moonlight

WHITE-WASHING THE WALLS
(For my mother)

"You just mix your sand with a little water . . ."

"How much?"

"Just enough to cover it, and when you put it on
always scoop enough sand in your water and keep
stirring and adding water. When you're ready to
start, at least say a few words to ask for help
and then it will go easier . . ."

this clay, sand-colored and dry, comes from a place near Laguna
the people have known about it for a long time

in a galvanized pan, mixed with warm water, I stir
and break up small hard chunks that crush easily
in my hands
an aroma like when it rains lightly, cool and sweet
fills the sunroom, taking me back years, to my mother's
house in Paguate, the adobe walls have always been
this color and always held this same smell
and in our small home among the grey sage
below Taos Mountain, it continues

TWENTY-FIRST OF MAY, 1981

moving through sunset's pastels
night settles calmly like a baby's breathing
a submissive sigh
and a moist southerly wind subsides in this place
where I've been told the "wind never blows"
two weeks ago I only dreamt of this home
being here is so much more

surrounded in thick seas of sage
broken only by a now-and-then
juniper struggling to send roots
through the un-yielding clay

to the west, running slow and deep
flows the powerful Rio Grande
sending our water messages swiftly
southward to the oceans
and oh, the stories your great waters
must tell these deep canyons
during the run-offs that never fail to come
late snows and early rains
being your only clock
the rhythmic flow of cold pendulum waters
rushing far below through ageless volcanic trails

I once brought a beautiful fish out of your depths
he was living beneath a sunken granite slab
and mistook my shiny lure for an intruder
entering his blue-green solitude
but I thanked you for him and
many people shared him with me
feasting on his happiness
knowing his life gave life

remembering now
how his body glistened while leaping
looking right through me with that round mystical eye
and gave himself to me only
after every possible ounce of fight withered
his smooth silver-blue sides
and the deep red flaring gills
rose and fell breathless
I yearn to return to your laughing waters
lying far beneath this sagey plateau
how will you welcome me?
I wait contented in knowing it will come
a re-kindling of that not-too-long-ago remembrance
brought on by this wonderous deep nightfall

WHIRLING

(For Tom Ehrlich)

listening to a master, this complex movement
of ivory and ebony touching flesh, communing
and the whirling rhythm of air
from a southeast corner of our home

mountainous clouds gathering
rush north, coming swiftly along a southern horizon
watch the rain form in dense blankets
swirling and building, layer upon layer
looking like horned bread of pueblo ovens
piled high and moving
traveling the huge opening-and-closing sky
far off the in the grey-blue mass
thunder plays back and forth unseen, rumbling
and moving as do your nimble fingers
striking keys lovingly and stirring the sound

and then the rain sprinkling
seen from miles away
as if a tumbling watery ball
rolls across the arid plain
its momentum changing constantly
like that of the piano you play
a cool misty spray precedes
wave after wave of dark rain clouds passing
briefly blocking warm rays of an afternoon sun

Taos Mountain, north in half shadow
where the storm centers
a patchwork quilt of clouds
wrapped around snow-tipped peaks

breathe deep
there is a lightness
a calming within
an intensity of peace
following with eyes and ears
the heart-song of the skies' Spring procession
and your flowing, laughing fingers

BUILDING A DREAM

(For Barbara, Nov. 1981)

alive in the arc of an evening double rainbow
visions flood my mind, recollecting warm days of early May
when our building began
the assurance of my builder friends, the hopefulness of Carl and I
hand digging the foundation on Mother's Day
how unaware you and I were of our own strengths and limits
testing our bodies and hearts with hard work
half-circled in the aura, head bowed I solemnly give my prayers
back to everything and everyone who shared in this work

Carl took me to the Mountain the day before we began
it was so easy to ask for help there in the surrounding beauty of
dense ponderosa, blue spruce and aspen
where tiny butterflies, irridescent blue and shimmering wove a
moving blanket of welcome as we passed quietly
entering deeper into the folds of the Mountain's belly
walking a well-worn footpath
there beside the Rio Lucero, wary cutthroat trout darted between
pools and riffles of the clear river making fluid momentary shadows
in the cold rippling water
we ate our lunch beneath the shade of a giant spruce and I wished
you were there sharing this spring afternoon with me
giving praise to all the creation and knowing the blessing returned

days later, we got Gilbert to haul the adobes in his two-ton flatbed
and Bunny helped too
Carl was eager then and the work slowly progressed through the late
afternoon hours of early summer's heat
beginning in the cool morning breezes I learned to mix mud
for him and Charles, while they steadily laid adobes listening to
old tapes hour after hour
Hank Williams and war dance songs from Rocky Boy and Bismark
kept us company till after sunset

in the warm evenings my tired arms and shoulders ached
my legs remained numb through long restful nights
I turned sun-bronzed as the weeks passed and Carl started calling me
a 'shit-colored Indin', my arms and legs grew accustomed to the
day's work and again it was easy to keep up and I thanked the land
for accepting us to this change

there was that day when Doug, Ev and their kids, my sister Gail,
Yazzie and Art arrived to help, I was even more excited seeing our
dream becoming real
the walls of the studio getting higher, window-level now, as we all
worked through dusk until light faded and wearily feasted on posole
sweet corn and melon, drank lots of Coors and wine, and laughed in
the lull of night watched over by a near round moon and thousands
of flickering stars

I met David, Arthur and James, lifetime friends who started a
lumber business at the pueblo
they brought our already cut vigas down from the mountains
hauled them out here where they lay peeled and curing
reflecting the sun like polished ivory
then there were many delays to get used to:
no workers showing up or no supplies in town or no money
we struggled along and somehow managed to make things work
even through the disappointments
beginning to understand our own place meshing with the rhythms
of the land
growing closer as a family in the life-giving breath of the Creator
His reminding presence all encompassing
beneath the roundness of this double rainbow

and there, in that moment, I found a home!
like the bullet's home deep in the chest
of the white-tail buck bounding
then stumbling and finally falling

IF YOU CAN HEAR MY HOOVES

if you can hear my hooves in crisp autum leaves
see my blue-grey body of winter
then you will know the songs in my heart
songs of my hunter heart
pulsing steadily with my eyes
awaiting the deer dancing with my spirit
pray there is that strength in me to bring him home

A GIFT FOR THE HUNTERS

a gift for the hunters
long awaited and prayed for . . .

winter comes whispering
rolling along in billowy woven grey shadow
racing East toward the Mountain
thunder-echoes rumble in half daylight, near and far
all is waiting for frozen flakes heavy clouds carry
hear the movement in our hearts and come!
bring forth your burdens, turn them to blessings
sprinkle them gently on a dark land and thirsty fallow fields
hear the people's singing
and now come whispering cold and wet
from a windy southern horizon
blowing away a lazy midday sun

HUNTER'S MORNING

I went out only once with my bow last year
high into the scattered snow mountains above Vallecitos and
did not get a deer but caught the before sunrise chill on my face
felt my weight break the still-frozen snow beneath my feet
looked back to see my prints just visible in the coming light
smelled a cool wetness of clear springs trickling in the dark
saw the outlines of tall ponderosa pine with ice-bent branches
quietly rustling in the wind's soft breathing as I climbed
still higher
stopped to catch my breath and heard two far-off crows caw
for the coming sun and was audience to coyotes barking
back and forth between unseen canyons
watched the blue-grey sky lighten and silent stars fade
felt cold Winter breezes numb my face while I sat shivering
on a rocky ledge overlooking a dim and hazy horizon
blew warm breath into my cupped hands and looked and listened
attentive, while the sun, now rising
cast patches of red and yellow light on distant blue mountains
walked as quietly as I could through dry scrub oak thickets
looking for fresh tracks and droppngs in the calm splendor of dawn
began to feel that warm glow run all through me
stopped and prayed, whispering gratitude for that one hunter's morning
held in memory

ALONE IS THE HUNTER

alone is the hunter
who seeks only to kill
and not reach into
what he has taken
and accept fully
all that is given

FOR LARRY

listening to sounds of Winter slowly fading
bringing closer the season for growing
recalling long ago, in Utah, with you in the crisp morning air
climbing and breathing hard up that steep Intermountain mountain
working our way up slowly
aware that dawn was coming quickly

lights from the school below
above, sage and box elder trees silhouetted against the night

in the morning chill our breaths could be seen blowing
as the sun woke up and climbed the mountain with us

I tired quickly and fell behind
among the slippery shale rock and thick grey sage
I could see you higher up and breathing heavy
and I tried to hurry and follow your steps
the day was warming, the frost melting
do you remember?

you waited for me near the top
and you didn't have to say "you all right?"

I was,
just a little out of breath
that moment something shined brightly in your eyes
you smiled, and it wasn't the sun breaking through the clouds
clouds, fluffy and dense, that cap the mountains in early autumn

we continued up and up
I tried to stay close
but you were more sure than me
and I lagged behind again

you were maybe fifty yards above me
all I could see was your back and
the long barrel of the rifle you carried
but I saw you slowly stop
you never looked to see me hurrying
but knew I was right behind when you whispered "wait"
I looked where you looked and then they moved
two dark bodies, almost grey, across the narrow canyon

all motion seemed so slow but I remember
you quietly crouched to sit
and rested the rifle on a rock
the shot broke the silence and cast echoes back and forth
all along the craggy peaks and between the oak-filled canyons below

then once again, all was quiet

the larger of the two grey forms stepped forward then dropped
and rolled noisily down into the oaks
the other knowingly waited
then moved cautiously up and over to the next ridge

we waited and watched below for some sign of movement
when there was none you eased your way down
looking for the blood you knew would be there
I remember you carried a pistol on your hip
I heard that go off with a sharp crack
that reverberated in the canyon bottoms

then you called just loud enough to hear
I almost ran down I was so excited
you stood beside her, bending to touch her head
the most beautiful doe I'd ever seen

we prayed to her and to everything all around

you mostly, because I didn't know about praying
I was learning and growing
when she was clean and rested
and we had eaten our apples and bread
you carried her down the mountain on your back
with me carrying your rifle following

and I watched her say good-bye to her mountain
to the trees she had slept under
to the springs she had drunk from so many times
to all her people in the mountains
with her sky blue eyes open
and her head bouncing lightly on your shoulder
I grew a little more that day and wanted to sing
but didn't know what to sing

you carried her so lightly and we were coming home
when we left her hidden in the trees by the road
you finally spoke:
"Boy, I hope Mom is cooking some fried potatoes,
c'mon, let's go."
and I fell twice, stumbling to keep up
as we made our way back down
the mountain at sundown
crossing fences, jumping irrigation ditches
running through melon fields
and finally walking the sun-soft asphalt of the school

when we were home and Mom sat with us eating liver and laughing
you looked at me and laughed because I was so tired
later that night we borrowed a car to bring the deer home
when she came into our house we dressed her and welcomed her
with those special things and prayed some more
and we talked, you and I, for a long time

I remember this, maybe I was twelve that fall, and you
came from New Mexico to be with us for a little while

Driving to Denver on U.S. 285
a song came to me
in those mountains south of Bailey
thought about Kenosha Pass
and that small herd of buffalo at Red Mountain
the way we saw them the first time
all huddled together in the blowing snow . . .

OLD MAN FOR HIS PEOPLE

(In memory of Alex Sherwood)

I remember still the meal we shared and
that time with you and your 'partner'
and the stories you told of how it was back then
bringing our lives, separated by many years, that much closer
you holding my children on your lap and laughing
and I remember the greeting for your sister and
her man in Chewelah when entering their house
how calm your handshake was when we first met
and your eyes that looked through me and cradled me
gently in wisdom and love

Old man for his people
watching us eternally
moving quietly among us
lending strength

it was with heart heavy in our home
that we heard of your passing
quietly reminiscing and grieving
we spoke of you and Margaret
and the days your stories recalled

of the berry picking feasts and camas gathering
of going many miles in the wagon to celebration
and playing stick game
of bringing home deer and making meat for the winter

Old man for his people
I hear you singing
not of the sorrow that finally took you
but of the happy days with your wife
and the things you shared

up there in the mountains that echo your voice
up there, blowing high above human ears
your medicine sings strong and good
for 'Children of the Sun'

I will pray, up there
in the mountains
that my own children
will not forget the song you sing

all of us who knew you
now know how much you are truly missed and loved
but ours here is to go on and
respect you daily
through the things that meant and mean
so much to you, Old man
it is not forgotten

in the clear mountain air
in the Spokane River rising
in the pine-filled forests
in the salmon swimming
in the white-tail bounding
and ruffed grouse calling
in the old men singing
and women dancing
will you be heard and
be forever with us, Grandfather

PENNSYLVANIA WINTER INDIAN 1974

like a woman you've longed to make love to, and finally did
was the warmth I bathed in, wandering through your land
where the colors of Winter unfold before you
like a rolled-out blanket
and the winds make forests bow
as they gently weave and spin their songs
through the open valleys and endless rolling hills
yellow grasses that stretch wide and far
against a pale blue sky
bordering the ever-present forests of thin dark trees
of which I know no name
clear running brooks and creeks that flow onward towards the sea
these are the faces of the woman I saw
her name, Pennsylvania
she sang to me in her sunlit days and I listened
hearing the life that abounds in her woods
the deer, the squirrels, each animal has a different song
it would take a lifetime to hear them all
but I remember most the sounds of her body moving
sighing, heaving, giving birth to Spring
ice in the rivers breaking into thousands of pieces flowing South
going home to the sea, and I too, like the rivers going home
flowing and running clean, remembering the woman of the East
in all I've seen

going home to my people, where life is flowing and forever
like the unbroken stillness of a cold Winter night
back to the country from which I came
back to the yucca, cedar and crooked piñon trees
but I will tell my people of this woman,
the country East, and I will say with song in my heart
*"country beautiful, now behind me, in my eyes and
ever in my heart"*
and they will know your land of which I speak
they will see as I saw all the greatness and
sincerity of Pennsylvania, the woman who cared
for her children and me, as one of her children
roaming, rambling and singing in her hills and
open valleys, bathing in all her beauty

COMING HOME IN MARCH

partying by a river near Ellwood City, Pennsylvania
getting loud and high
keeping company with people I met
empty cans of past party-ers and broken glass
a song from numbed mouth coming out
weakly bouncing back through the quiet
we all stood by the tracks and laughed at my song
"hey little Indian, sing that again"
"yeah bird, again"
song building
louder, clearer
"that's far-out, man"
"you're all right, Littlebird, right-on"
"yeah far-out, bird"
. . . away in winter
when men of the pueblo, young and old
sing the season, and the village echoes the heart throb
of the drum beating strong . . .
a wind in the trees
moon climbing high
stars shining brightly through cloudless sky
singing my heart deep into the night
holding on, remembering
lump in my throat growing harder

BENEATH RAINBOWS

(For Randy Silva May 2, 1980)

it's about a two hour drive from Taos Pueblo to Santa Fe
the afternoon sun casts broken light, here and there
desperately trying to break through dark rain-filled clouds
forming heavy in the west
coming away from the village
we pass the men gathered in an open field
sitting, waiting
wrapped in faded cotton blankets
perhaps talking about someone's horse
that was hit by a car last night or
maybe asking about a relative's field, yet to be planted
sharing stories
the men are gathering
each quietly thinking to himself and
staring at the small fire
with its thin wisp of smoke rising lazily
unbothered by any sign of wind
I look back one last time before we round a curve
and then they are no longer within the eyes' reach
Randy talks first:
"Just think, long time ago, there was no road here
those men would be sitting in this field
no telephone wires or fences
they don't care about the road, telephone wires or the tourists
gawking and taking pictures, they are waiting . . .

waiting to see who among them will be chosen,
for tomorrow, to represent the people.
You should see them in the fall, during San Geronimo
the bright colored blankets and Mexican serapes
and the colors of the field and trees
Have you ever seen the races?"
"No, I haven't. When I was in high school
my roommate, Carl, was always asking me to come up
but I never did. But I sure want to."
"You should, it's really something.
It's like our feast days, when we take part
all the preparing, the work, the care, you know."

we stop in town, pick up a six-pack, head south
through Rancho de Taos and on into the steep canyon
working our way down
winding our way towards the river
passing Embudo
talking and laughing, sharing memories of our own feast days
Randy talks of growing up and dancing
and the children now
"I hope we can pass these things on to the kids,
to help them remember, so they will understand."
"Yeah", I say, "to help them grow and know where
they come from, so they can in turn work hard
for the people."
Randy's voice unhurried and calm:

"It's hard to be Indian."
I look at him and nod
and I drift back through the mind's eye
the Taos men gathered in the field
waiting to be chosen
the weeks spent in preparing, the sacrifice
and I see myself also, during our feast
one among many dancing for all the people
the food, the laughter, the being together.

we're almost in Española now
that stretch of prairie dog town just outside
and it begins to rain
not hard, just enough to use the windshield wipers, off and on
past San Juan, a breeze gently blows and
the wind carries that sweet rain smell to us
the smell of the land being washed lovingly by unseen hands
we roll down our windows and breath deep
thankful for the blessing

we laugh about the jokes the old men tell
when we gather, when it's our turn to take part
and then we're in Pojoaque at the 7 to 11
pull up beside my truck and talk a little longer
Randy leaves as I start my truck
he drives north, back to Santa Clara
I go south still headed towards Santa Fe

I smile thinking of all we talked about
and the things we share
a song bounces off thick black clouds
hovering above Camel Rock
bursts from my parched throat and
thunder rolls all around me
rain pouring across the land in cleansing waves
"whu-eh!"
singing easily I descend Big Tesuque hill into town
catch the truck by-pass on St. Francis Drive
reach the intersection of Cordova and St. Francis
as the traffic light changes to yellow and
quickly speed through,
along with all the other five o'clock people
rushing home
get caught in the left hand lane, stopped behind a red light
waiting for the green
look to the east, through the steady drizzle
towards the park where all the children are playing
some kicking soccer balls
some practising ground strokes on the tennis courts
others chasing 'grounders' with baseball gloves
hear the laughter of the children
above the drone of the cars idleing
and above them forming perfect arches
enclosing the children, running, chasing unaware
are two luminous rainbows

one full color and radiant in the clear wet air
the other lightly faded and dimmer
but two incredible full rainbows covering
with hope and prayer
the children in all that innocence
my breathing tightens, a hard lump grows in my throat
and tears blur my eyes and I whisper
"let it be so."
the light turns green, traffic begins to move
I shift into first and begin to creep forward
turning my head, straining to hold onto that vision
just a little longer

cars thin out as I work my way toward the I-25 ramp
south to Albuquerque
songs from rock, from tree and grass
from milky white clouds
fill the cool after-rain air with sound
during a momentary pause between songs I slow down
make the circular turn underneath all three overpasses
to the two-laned Madrid highway
my eyes squinting from the brightness
of the wet, cleansed land
over the bridge, up the hill and
onto the slippery muddy road, last quarter mile
pools of murky rain water lining both sides

past the iron gate, bouncing through the ruts
sliding from side to side
careful not to slip into the ditch
pull up to the faded orange stucco house
and slide to a stop in the thick brown mud
even before I'm out, Maya, barefoot and grinning
greets me from the doorway with "Hi, Daddy!"
Barbara smiles and opens the screen door
I hear Randy's voice reminding
quietly moving within me,
"I hope we can pass these things on to the children."
I enter thinking: *"To help them grow and
know where they come from."*

An edition of 750 copies set in 10 point
Bembo using Warren's Antique Book Paper,
printed by West Coast Print
Center & published by
Tooth of Time Books
634 E. Garcia,
Santa Fe
New Mexico
87501

*

Grateful
acknowledgement
to the National Endowment
for the Arts
for their kind assistance

*

We encourage bookstores
to order direct from our distributors:
Book People: 2940 Seventh St., Berkeley, Ca. 94710
Inland Book Co.: P.O. Box 261, East Haven, Ct. 06512